Charm is deceptive, and beauty does not last; but a woman who fears the LORD will be greatly praised. Reward her for all she has done. Let her deeds publicly declare her praise.

Proverbs 31:30–31 NLT

A MOTHER'S GIFT OF Love

a keepsake of quotes, prayers, and
scriptures in celebration of motherhood

BLUE SKY INK.

Brentwood, Tennessee

The only thing that counts is *faith* expressing itself through *love*.

Galations 5:6 NIV

No language can express the

power and *beauty* and

heroism of a

mother's love.

Edwin H. Chapin

Love flashes like fire,

the brightest kind of flame.

Many waters cannot quench love;

neither can rivers drown it.

Song of Songs 8:6–7 NLT

love

Mother *love* is the fuel that enables

normal human being to do the impossible

Marion C. Garrety

Love never gives up,

never loses faith, is always

hopeful, and endures through

every circumstance.

1 Corinthians 13:7 NLT

Love comes from God and those who are loving and kind show that they are the children of God, and that they are getting to know him better.

1 John 4:7 TLB

heart

There is none in all this

cold and hollow world,

No fount of deep, strong,

deathless love,

Like that within a ***mother's heart***.

Mrs. Hemans (Felicia Dorothea Browne)

A mother's *love* endures through all; in good repute, in bad repute, in the face of the world's condemnation, a mother still loves on. She . . . remembers the infant *smiles* . . . the joyful shout of childhood . . . the promise of his youth; and she can never be brought to think him all unworthy.

Washington Irving

There is no *greater* place of ministry,

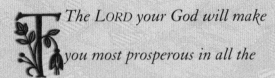

The Lord your God will make you most prosperous in all the work of your hands and in the fruit of your womb.

Deuteronomy 30:9 NIV

position, or power than that of a *mother.*

Phil Whisenhunt

Since future victory is sure, be strong and steady, always abounding in the LORD's work for you know that nothing you do for the Lord is ever wasted.

1 Corinthians 15:58 TLB

The memory of my *mother* and her teachings were after all the only capital I had to start life with, and on that capital I have made my way.

Andrew Jackson

All your children shall be taught by the LORD, And great shall be the peace of your children.

Isaiah 54:13 NKJV

my mother

My *mother* was the making of me.

She was so true and so sure of me

I felt I had something to *live* for—someone

I must not disappoint. The memory of my

mother will always be a blessing to me.

Thomas A. Edison

Countless times each day

a *mother* . . . teaches,

ministers, *loves*, and nurtures

the *next* generation of citizens.

James C. Dobson and Gary L. Bauer

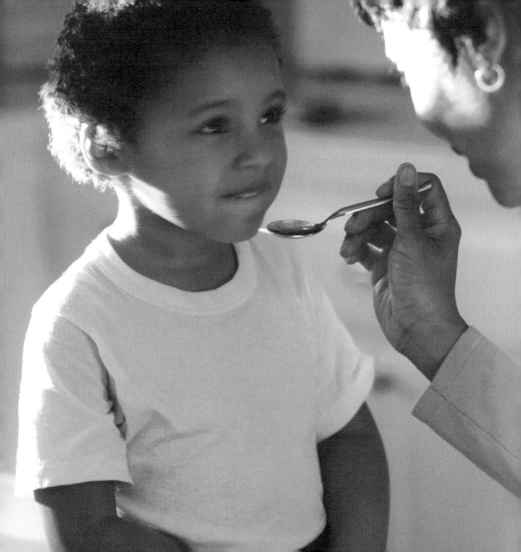

"Isn't there one child you really *love* the best?"

a mother was asked. And she replied, " Yes.

The one who is *sick* until he gets *well*;

the one who's *away*, until she gets *home*."

Wisdom is a tree of life to those who embrace her;
happy are those who hold her tightly.

Proverbs 3:18 NLT

God sought to give the *sweetest* thing

in his almighty power

To earth; and *deeply* pondering

what it should be one hour

In fondest joy and *love* of heart

outweighing every other,

He moved the gates of *heaven* apart

and gave to earth a mother.

mother

A mother is not

a person to lean on

but a person to make

leaning unnecessary.

Dorothy Canfield Fisher

Point your kids in the right direction—
when they're old they won't be lost.

Proverbs 22:6 THE MESSAGE

Don't neglect your mother's teaching. What you learn from them will crown you with grace and clothe you with honor.

Proverbs 1:8–9 NLT

Some are *kissing* mothers and some are scolding mothers, but it is *love* just the same, and most mothers *kiss* and scold together.

Pearl S. Buck

A mother is God's deputy on earth!

Rachel L. Varnhagen

Discipline isn't much fun. It always feels like it's going against the grain. Later, of course, it pays off handsomely, for it's the well-trained who find themselves mature in their relationship with God.

Hebrews 12:11 THE MESSAGE

I remember my *mother's prayers* and they have always followed me. They have clung to me all my *life*.

Samuel Taylor Coleridge

Prayer is the application of

the *heart* to God, and the

internal exercise of *love.*

Samuel Taylor Coleridge

The eyes of the LORD are on the righteous

and his ears are attentive to their prayer.

1 Peter 3:12 NIV

Most of all the other *beautiful*

things in life come by twos and threes,

by dozens and hundreds. Plenty of

roses, stars, sunsets, rainbows,

brothers and sisters, aunts and cousins,

but only one *mother* in the whole world.

Kate Douglas Wiggin

The *power* of one

mother's prayers could

stand an army on its ear.

Elizabeth DeHaven

Jesus said, *"If you believe, you will receive*

whatever you ask for in prayer."

Matthew 21:22 NIV

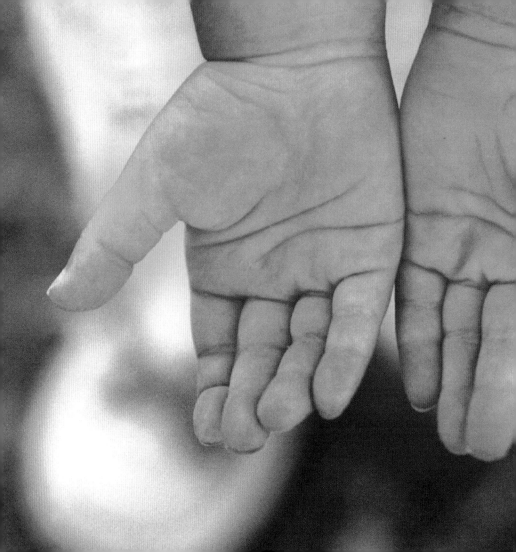

Hannah said, "I asked the LORD to give me this child, and he has given me my request. Now I am giving him to the LORD, and he will belong to the LORD his whole life."

1 Samuel 1:27–28 NLT

Stories first heard at a *mother's* knee

are never wholly forgotten—a little

spring that never quite dries up in our

journey through scorching years.

Giovanni Ruffini

When [a good woman] speaks she has something

worthwhile to say and she always says it kindly.

Proverbs 31:26 THE MESSAGE

There is no velvet so soft as a mother's lap, no rose as lovely as her smile,

no path so flowery as that imprinted with her footsteps. —Archibald Thompson

Dissect a *mother's* heart and see the properties it doth contain—what pearls of *love*, what gems of *hope*. A mother's heart beats not in vain.

Caleb Dunn

A mother is . . . one who can take the place

mother's love

Youth fades; *love* droops;

the leaves of friendship fall;

A *mother's* secret love

outlives them all.

Oliver Wendell Holmes

of all others, but whose place no one else can take. —G. Mermillod

A mother's love for the *child* of her body

differs essentially from all other affections,

and burns with so *steady* and clear a flame

that it appears like the one unchangeable

thing in this earthly mutable *life*, so that

when she is no longer present

it is still a *light* to our steps

and a consolation.

W. H. Hudson

A Mother's Gift of Love
ISBN 1-59475-026-2

Copyright © 2004 by GRQ, Inc.
Brentwood, Tennessee 37027

Published by Blue Sky Ink, a division of GRQ, Inc.
Brentwood, Tennessee 37027

Scripture quotations noted TLB are from *The Living Bible*, copyright ©
1971. Used by permission of Tyndale House Publishers, Inc., Wheaton,
Illinois 60189. All rights reserved.

Scripture quotations noted THE MESSAGE are from *The Message*. Copyright
© by Eugene H. Peterson 1993, 1994, 1995, 1996, 2000. Used by permission of NavPress Publishing Group. All rights reserved.

Scripture quotations noted NIV are taken from the Holy Bible: New
International Version®. NIV®. Copyright © 1973, 1978, 1984, by the
International Bible Society. Used by permission of Zondervan Publishing
House. All rights reserved.

Scripture quotations noted NKJV are taken from the Holy Bible, New King
James Version. Copyright © 1982 by Thomas Nelson, Inc. Used by permission. All rights reserved.

Scripture quotations noted NLT are from the *Holy Bible, New Living
Translation*, copyright © 1996. Used by permission of Tyndale House
Publishers, Inc., Wheaton, Illinois 60189. All rights reserved.

Editor: Lila Empson
Compiler: Snapdragon Editorial Group, Inc., Tulsa, Oklahoma
Design: Diane Whisner, Tulsa, Oklahoma

Printed in China.